WELCOME TO
SPAIN

COUNTRIES OF THE WORLD

Spain

by Shannon Anderson

BLASTOFF! READERS
2

BELLWETHER MEDIA • MINNEAPOLIS, MN

Blastoff! Readers are carefully developed by literacy experts to build reading stamina and move students toward fluency by combining standards-based content with developmentally appropriate text.

LEVELS

Level 1 provides the most support through repetition of high-frequency words, light text, predictable sentence patterns, and strong visual support.

Level 2 offers early readers a bit more challenge through varied sentences, increased text load, and text-supportive special features.

Level 3 advances early-fluent readers toward fluency through increased text load, less reliance on photos, advancing concepts, longer sentences, and more complex special features.

★ **Blastoff! Universe**

Reading Level

Grade K

Grades 1–3

Grade 4

This edition first published in 2024 by Bellwether Media, Inc.

No part of this publication may be reproduced in whole or in part without written permission of the publisher. For information regarding permission, write to Bellwether Media, Inc., Attention: Permissions Department, 6012 Blue Circle Drive, Minnetonka, MN 55343.

Library of Congress Cataloging-in-Publication Data

Names: Anderson, Shannon, 1972- author.
Title: Spain / by Shannon Anderson.
Description: Minneapolis, MN : Bellwether Media, 2024. | Series: Blastoff! Readers: Countries of the World | Includes bibliographical references and index. | Audience: Ages 5-8 | Audience: Grades 2-3 | Summary: "Relevant images match informative text in this introduction to Spain. Intended for students in kindergarten through third grade"– Provided by publisher.
Identifiers: LCCN 2023003564 (print) | LCCN 2023003565 (ebook) | ISBN 9798886874327 (library binding) | ISBN 9798886876208 (ebook)
Subjects: LCSH: Spain–Juvenile literature.
Classification: LCC DP17 .A657 2024 (print) | LCC DP17 (ebook) | DDC 946-dc23/eng/20230127
LC record available at https://lccn.loc.gov/2023003564
LC ebook record available at https://lccn.loc.gov/2023003565

Text copyright © 2024 by Bellwether Media, Inc. BLASTOFF! READERS and associated logos are trademarks and/or registered trademarks of Bellwether Media, Inc.

Editor: Rebecca Sabelko   Designer: Gabriel Hilger

Printed in the United States of America, North Mankato, MN.

Table of Contents

All About Spain	4
Land and Animals	6
Life in Spain	12
Spain Facts	20
Glossary	22
To Learn More	23
Index	24

All About Spain

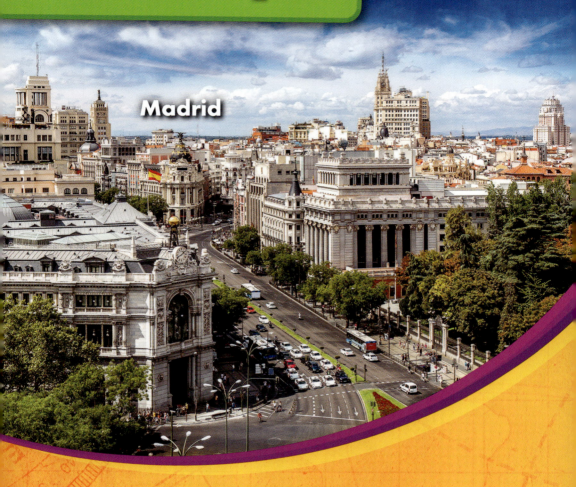

Madrid

Spain is a large country in southwestern Europe. Its capital is Madrid.

Spain makes up most of the Iberian **Peninsula**.

Land and Animals

The Meseta Central covers most of Spain. Mountains rise around much of this **plateau**.

Beaches line many coasts. Islands lie in nearby waters. Rivers flow throughout the country.

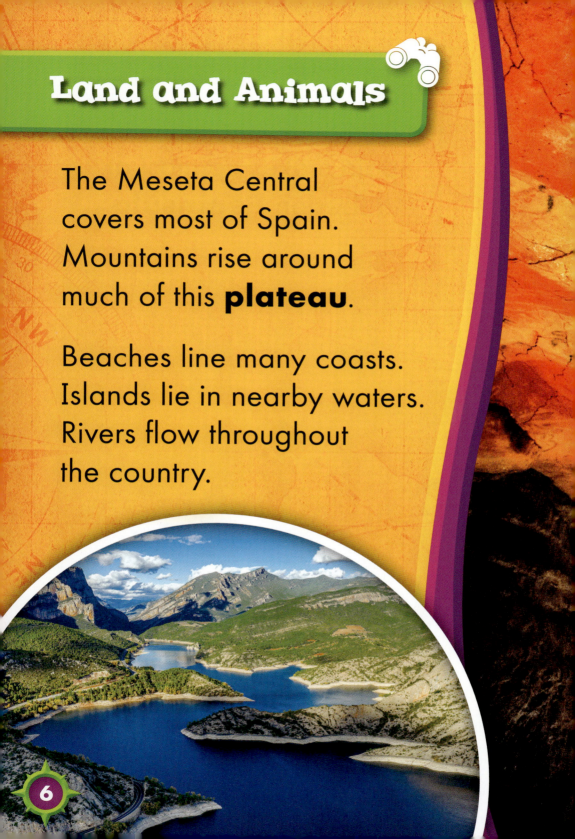

Cave of Altamira

Size: 971 feet (296 meters) long
Famous For: home to some of the earliest cave art ever discovered

Northern Spain can be cool and rainy. Snow falls on the mountains in the winter.

Southern Spain has wet winters. Summers are hot and dry.

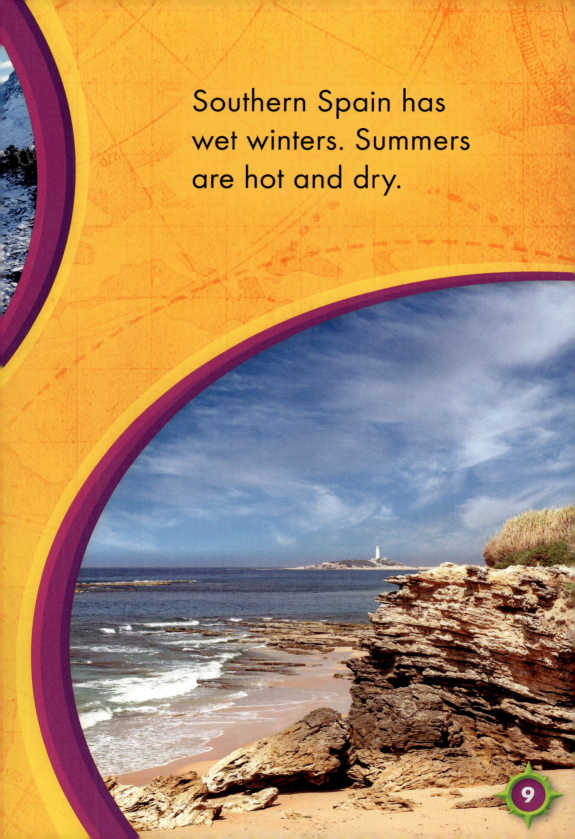

Dolphins swim along coasts. Wolves hunt deer in the northern forests.

Iberian wolf

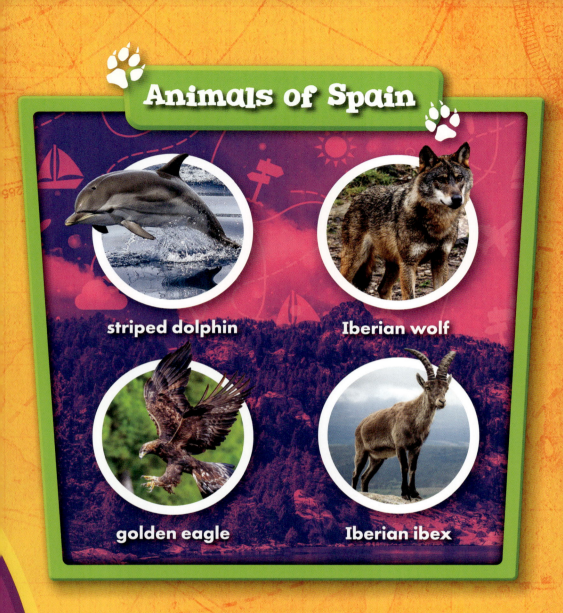

Animals of Spain

striped dolphin

Iberian wolf

golden eagle

Iberian ibex

Golden eagles fly over southern mountains. Ibex climb the rocky **slopes**.

Life in Spain

Most people speak Spanish. People often speak the language of their **region**, too.

Over half of all people in Spain are **Catholics**.

La Sagrada Família
Catholic church

Many people play soccer and basketball. They also like a type of racquetball called *jai alai*.

People enjoy motor sports and surfing. Folk arts are common in many regions.

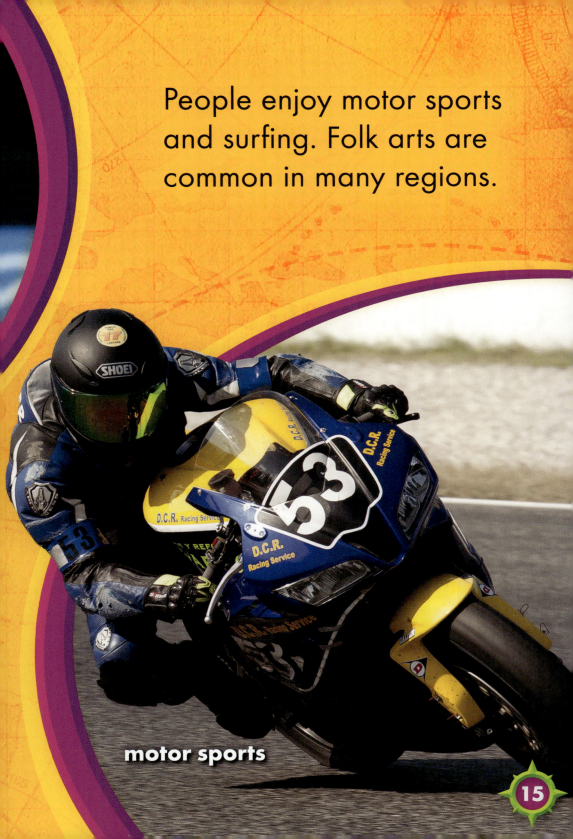

motor sports

Gazpacho and *paella* are popular meals in Spain.

Spanish Foods

gazpacho

paella

mushrooms in garlic sauce

octopus in paprika sauce

paella

Tapas are small plates served between meals. Some include mushrooms in garlic sauce. Octopus in paprika sauce is common, too.

People enjoy parades during the springtime festival *Las Fallas*.

Fiesta de San Fermín is in July. Fireworks light up the sky. People **celebrate** all year long!

Spain Facts

Size:
195,124 square miles
(505,370 square kilometers)

Population:
47,163,418 (2022)

National Holiday:
National Day (October 12)

Main Language:
Spanish

Capital City:
Madrid

Famous Face

Name: Sandra Sánchez Jaime

Famous For: Olympic karate gold medal winner

Religions

- other: 26%
- Atheist: 16%
- Roman Catholic: 58%

Top Landmarks

Alhambra

La Sagrada Família

Museo del Prado

Glossary

Catholics—people belonging or relating to the Christian church that is led by the pope

celebrate—to do something special or fun for an event, occasion, or holiday

peninsula—a section of land that extends out from a larger piece of land and is almost completely surrounded by water

plateau—an area of flat, raised land

region—a part of a country

slopes—the sides of hills or mountains

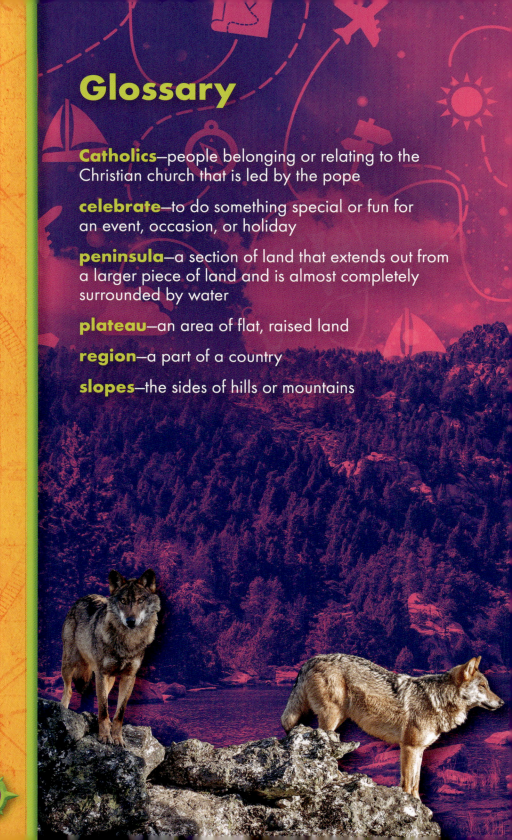

To Learn More

AT THE LIBRARY

Duling, Kaitlyn. *Alpine Ibex*. Minneapolis, Minn.: Bellwether Media, 2021.

Sebra, Richard. *Paella*. Minneaplis, Minn.: Pop!, 2021.

Spanier, Kristine. *Spain*. Minneapolis, Minn.: Jump!, 2020.

ON THE WEB

FACTSURFER

Factsurfer.com gives you a safe, fun way to find more information.

1. Go to www.factsurfer.com.

2. Enter "Spain" into the search box and click 🔍.

3. Select your book cover to see a list of related content.

Index

animals, 10, 11
basketball, 14
capital (see Madrid)
Catholics, 12
Cave of Altamira, 7
coasts, 6, 10
Europe, 4
Fiesta de San Fermín, 19
folk arts, 15
food, 16, 17
forests, 10
Iberian Peninsula, 5
islands, 6
jai alai, 14
Las Fallas, 18
Madrid, 4, 5
map, 5
Meseta Central, 6
motor sports, 15
mountains, 6, 8, 11
people, 12, 14, 15, 18, 19
rain, 8
rivers, 6
say hello, 13
snow, 8
soccer, 14
Spain facts, 20–21
Spanish, 12, 13
summer, 9
surfing, 15
winter, 8, 9

The images in this book are reproduced through the courtesy of: Mistervlad, front cover; Ivan Soto Cobos, front cover; Digoarpi, pp. 2-3; Alfonso de Tomas, p. 3; Sergii Figurnyi, pp. 4-5; KarSol, p. 6; Sergi Reboredo/ Alamy, pp. 6-7; ikumaru, pp. 8-9; Pacorpi, p. 9; J.M.Abarca, pp. 10-11; Gonzalo Jara, p. 11 (striped dolphin); Irene Castro Moreno, p. 11 (Iberian wolf); Svitlana Tkach, p. 11 (golden eagle); Nik Bruining, p. 11 (Iberian ibex); dimbar76, p. 12; Morsa Images, pp. 12-13; ph.FAB, pp. 14-15; Ricardo Hernandez, p. 14 (*jai alai*); Ivan Garcia, p. 15; Pixel-Shot, p. 16 (*gazpacho*); nelea33, p. 16 (*paella*); from my point of view, p. 16 (mushrooms in garlic sauce); Miguel Tamayo Fotografia, p. 16 (octopus in paprika sauce); Ollyy, p. 17; Pecold, pp. 18-19; titoOnz, p. 20 (flag); Aflo Co. Ltd./ Alamy, p. 20 (Sandra Sánchez Jaime); Taiga, p. 21 (*Alhambra*); 135pixels, p. 21 (*La Sagrada Família*); Sean Pavone, p. 21 (*Museo del Prado*); Ramon Carretero, p. 22.